THE TRIBAL PASHTUNS AFRIDIS

GOLU KUMAR

Copyright © Golu Kumar
All Rights Reserved.

The tribal Pashtuns of Pakistan, who live along the Afghan–Pakistan border, have long been stereotyped as "violent" and "warrior-like" in colonial and modern literature. A survey of archival literature, however, reveals that oriental representations of tribal Pashtuns are based on different generalizations established and perpetuated during British military missions against tribal Pashtuns. Furthermore, prejudices and generalizations about tribal Pashtuns have remained despite Pakistan's independence in 1947. Recent events in Pakistan's Pashtun tribal belt, with numerous tribes calling Jirga meetings, criticizing and fighting militant actions, and protesting against the state's injustices, demonstrate the tribal Pashtuns' importance and desire for peace. Finally, a quick examination of the Pashtun Tahafuz (protection) movement, which was recently launched (PTM), an indigenous peace and human rights organization that includes both men and women, and its peaceful nature strengthens the tribal Pashtuns' value of peace.

Contents

Foreword

DECLARATION

The purpose of this book is not to tell any particular caste religion as big or small, nor to reach the feelings of any particular caste or religion, the book is meant to be read-only.

CHAPTER ONE

AFRIDIS

The Afridis are a large tribe, inhabiting the lower and easternmost
spurs of the Safed Koh Range, to the west and south of the Peshawar
district, including the Bazar and Bara Valleys. On the east they are
bounded by British territory; on their north, they have the Mohmands;
west, the Shinwaris; and south, the Orakzais and Bangash.

Their origin is very obscure; Bellew identifies them with one of the
peoples referred to by Herodotus; their traditions, however, says James,
would lead us to believe that, in common with other Pathan tribes, they
are the descendants of Khalid-ibn-Walid, a Jew, who embraced Islamism,
and whose descendants had possession of great tracts in the western
a portion of Afghanistan during the tenth century. At this time, upon the
convulsions in the country owing to the advance of Mahmud of Ghazni, a

a chief named Afraid was obliged, owing to his enormities and feuds, to fly

from his country and seek refuge with a kindred spirit, by the name of Wazir,

in the wilds of Shir-i-Talla. Here he seems to have settled and to have

remained with his family for a considerable time. Turner gives something

of the same story, viz. that Afraid, an individual of unknown country and

parentage came to Ghor, and there had an intrigue with a woman of the

Karera tribe, the eventual result of which was the tribe of Afridis.

Cavagnari says of their origin that they are supposed to have been

descended from a woman named Maimana, who had two sons, Afraid and Adam.

But it is probably sufficient to surmise that they are a tribe of

Partisan stock, which has been established in their present country for

many centuries—far longer than the majority of Pathan tribes—and that

living as they do on the high road from Central Asia to India, it is

likely that they have a large admixture of Turkish and Scythian blood.

The Afridi country is bleak and sterile, and the rainfall but small,

agriculture is only scantily pursued, although they raise a coarse kind

of rice in the Bara Valley, a considerable amount of which

finds its way

to the Peshawar market. Some of the tribe also gain a precarious living

by cutting and selling timber for firewood, but many of the clans

possess great stock in cattle, cows, sheep, and goats, and go in for

breeding mules and donkeys, which are much thought of locally. Their

chief manufactures are coarse mats and cloth, while in Maidan, at

Imgur near Fort Bara, and in the Kohat Pass there are factories which

annually turn out a certain number of rifles.

[Sidenote: As Soldiers]

The Afridi in appearance is generally a fine, tall, athletic highlander,

whose springy step at once denotes his mountain origin. They are lean

but muscular men, with long, gaunt faces, high noses, and cheekbones, and

rather fair complexions. Brave and hardy, they make good soldiers, but

are apt to be somewhat homesick in the hot weather, and they have gained

a greater reputation for fidelity as soldiers than in any other way. The

Afridi has uniformly shown himself ready to enlist in our army, and at

At the present moment, there are probably 4000 of this tribe serving in the

ranks of the Indian army or in the Khyber Rifles. But since the Pathan is notoriously restless and dislikes expatriation, the average length of

service is shorter than in the case of our other Indian soldiers; the

the result is that a greater number of trained soldiers from Pathan

squadrons and companies annually pass back to their homes, then is the

case with a proportionately larger establishment of any other race.

While, therefore, their loyalty, while actually in our service and even

during frontier expeditions against their kinsmen, has been all that

could be wished, it is not perhaps saying much—considering their normal

family relations—that they should cheerfully fight for us against them.

But, on the other hand, it can hardly be expected that men who have

become again merged in their tribe, and who, according to their own

ideas are no longer bound to us by any obligation, should maintain an

the attitude of complete aloofness from any tribal movement prompted by

racial feeling, or by that fanaticism which, on the border, has been

defined as "a sentiment of religious intolerance excited into reckless

action." During the Tirah Campaign the number of pensioners and

reservists who fought against our troops are believed to

have been very
large. As long ago as 1884 it was stated by the Afridis that "almost
every fighting man possesses a gun or pistol, besides other arms; many
of the firearms are rifled, and some have percussion locks." To-day the
armament of these tribesmen is far more complete and up-to-date,[102]
and there can be no doubt that the fighting powers of the Afridis have
increased during recent years to a very formidable extent. At the same
the time our powers of effectively dealing with them have increased in a
still greater ratio. Our soldiers are more suitably trained for the
particular warfare waged in these border hills; they are infinitely
better armed; the services of transport and supply are more efficiently
organized; the country of the independent tribesmen is more thoroughly
known; the moral effect of uniformly successful expeditions—are all
factors that more than counterbalance any accession of strength which
the last twenty-five years have brought to the Afridis.

As to the measures to be taken effectually to coerce them, Oliver,
writing twenty-two years ago, said that "strong as are the natural
positions they hold among the spurs and defiles of the

Safed Koh and the

bare, rugged, inhospitable ranges of the Khyber; difficult to approach

the passes which might have to be forced, and unanimous as the clans may

be to defend them at the signal of a common danger, the people are so

dependent on the plains, their position—secure though it may sound—is

their weakest point, and makes it easy to shut them up in their

own hills. Peshawar, the great field for their plundering operations, is

also the market for their products and the source of supply for their

many domestic wants. Exclusion from Peshawar is to many clans a severe

form of punishment; and an effectual blockade that will cut them off

from the outer world, would probably bring them to terms sooner than an

expedition." But Holdich again reminds us that "across those wild

break-neck passes over the Safed Koh into Ningrahar ... the hard-pressed

Afridi can constantly find refuge for his family and sanctuary for

himself, amongst the Durani tribes who dwell on the northern slopes of

the Safed Koh." That there is always that back door, "the keys of which

are in their own pockets," and that "at the worst, they could shift

across the hills into Afghanistan, and there was the
prospect ... that
something more than mere shelter would be accorded by
the ruler of
Kabul."

[Sidenote: Their Character]

Of the moral attributes of the Afridis few people have
found much to say
in praise. Mackeson wrote of them: "The Afridis are a most
avaricious
race, desperately fond of money. Their fidelity is measured
by the
length of the purse of the seducer, and they transfer their
obedience
and support from one party to another of their clansmen,
according
to the comparative liberality of the donation." Elphinstone,
generally
ready enough to record anything good of Afghans, said of
the Afridis:
"On the whole, they are the greatest robbers among the
Afghans, and, I
imagine, have no faith or sense of honor; for I never heard
of anybody
hiring an escort of Khaiberis to secure his passage through
their
country—a step which always ensures a traveler's safety in
the lands of
any other tribe." MacGregor considers this estimate harsh,
but that
furnished by the same authority is hardly more flattering:
"A ruthless,
cowardly robber—a cold-blooded treacherous murderer;

brought up from his
earliest childhood amid scenes of appalling treachery and merciless
revenge, nothing has changed him; as he has lived—a shameless, cruel
savage—so he dies. And it would seem that, notwithstanding his long
intercourse with us, and the fact that large numbers have been and are
in our service, and must have learned in some way what faith, justice, and
mercy mean, yet the Afridi is no better than in the days of his father."

Against these adverse testimonies, however, there is the opinion of Sir
Robert Warburton, who spent eighteen years in their midst and who wrote
of them: "The Afridi lad from his earliest childhood is taught by the
circumstances of his existence and life to distrust all mankind, and
very often his near relations, heirs to his small plot of land by
inheritance, are his deadliest enemies. Therefore, distrust of all mankind and
readiness to strike the first blow for the safety of his own life has
become the Afridi's maxims. If you can overcome this
mistrust, and be kind in words to him, he will repay you by great
devotion, and he will put up with any punishment you like to give him
except abuse. It took me years to get through this thick

crust of
mistrust, but what was the after-result? For upwards of
fifteen years, I
went about unarmed amongst these people. Whenever it
happened
to be pitched, my camp was always guarded and protected
by them. The deadliest
enemies of the Khyber range, with a long record of blood
feuds, dropped
those feuds for the time being when in my camp. The
property was always
safe... Time after time have the Afridi elders and jirgas
supported me
even against their Maliks."

[Sidenote: Warburton's Opinion]

Notwithstanding all that has been said against the
Afridi, he is, on the
whole, one of the finest of the Pathan races on our border.
His
appearance is greatly in his favor, and he is braver, more
open,
and not more treacherous than many other Pathans. This
much is certain,
that he has the power of prejudicing Englishmen in his
favor, and there
are few brought into contact with him who does not at least
begin with
enthusiastic admiration for his manliness. Again, with a
tight hand over
him, many of his faults remain dormant, and he soon
develops into a
valuable soldier.

Though eternally at feud among themselves, they seldom quarrel with
neighboring tribes; that is, the Afridis do not care to waste their
energies in fighting with their neighbors, but reserve the luxury for
home consumption—a feud to an Afridi is the salt of life, the one
pleasure that makes existence tolerable. On occasion, in the face of
common danger, they are capable of concerted action, as was shown in the
Tirah Campaign of 1897, but even then one clan held entirely aloof.
Though nominally under the control of their Maliks, the Afridis have
very little respect for their authority and are thoroughly democratic.
They are all of the Sunni persuasion of the Muhammadan faith.

The following are the eight clans into which the Afridi tribe is
divided, and of these, the first six are known collectively as the
"Khyber Afridis":

1. Kuki Khel.
2. Malikdin Khel.
3. Kambar Khel.
4. Kamrai or Kamar Khel.
5. Zakha Khel.
6. Sipah.
7. Aka Khel.
8. Adam Khel.

The _Aka Khels_ have no connection with the Khyber and are located to
the south of the Bara River. The _Adam Khels_ inhabit the hills between
the districts of Kohat and Peshawar, and cannot be regarded, except
ethnologically, as a part of the Afridi tribe; for whether they are
viewed concerning their position, their interests, or their
habits, they are a distinct community.

The area of the country inhabited by the Afridis is about nine hundred
square miles. The principal streams draining their hills are the
northern branch of the Bara River, or Bara proper, the Bazar or Chora
River, and the Khyber stream, all flowing into the Peshawar Valley. The
valleys lying near the sources of the Bara River are included in the
general name of Tirah, which comprises an area of 600 to 700 square
miles. The greater part of Tirah is inhabited by different clans of the
Orakzai tribe, but the valleys known as Rajgal and Maidan are occupied
by the Afridis. The Rajgal Valley is drained by one mainstream, into
which fall some lesser streams from the surrounding hills. Its length is
about ten miles, and the breadth of the open country about four to five
miles. The elevation is over 5000. Maidan lies to the south

of Rajgal

and is a circular valley about ten miles across, watered by several

large watercourses. The streams from Rajgal and Maidan unite and form

the Bara River, flowing down the valley of the same name to the Kajurai

Plain, shortly before entering which the Bara is joined by the Mastura

River.

[Sidenote: The Clans]

The _Kuki Khel_ number some 5600 fighting men, and occupy the Rajgal

valley and the eastern end of the Khyber Pass, as far as the Rohtas

Hill, which overhangs the fort at Ali Musjid, and also the Bezai Spur—a

long under feature which flanks, but at a considerable distance, the

the latter part of the railway and road from Peshawar to Fort Jamrud. This

the clan has a bitter feud with the Zakha Khel and is Gar in politics.

The _Malikdin Khel_ is the Khan Khel or head clan of the Afridis and is

closely connected with the Kambar Khel, their settlements in Maidan,

Chora and Kajurai lie together. In Maidan, they occupy the central and

the northern portion of the valley—Bagh, the recognized meeting place of the

Afridi Jirgahs, "where the Khyber raid and Afridi rebellion of 1897–98 were planned, and where fanaticism, intrigue, and sedition have always

been hot-bedded and nourished," being in their country. The Malik

Keys number some 6000 fighting men and are Samil in politics.

The _Kambar Khel_ is numerically the most powerful of all the Afridi

clans, being able in an emergency to put 10,000 armed men in the field;

they belong to the Gar political faction. This clan is very migratory,

occupying in the hot weather the Kahu Darra and the valley of the

Shalobar River, which joins the Bara River at Dwatoi, and moves in the

winter to the Kajurai Plain and other minor settlements. This clan is

very strongly represented in the Indian Army and Border Militia.

The _Kamrai_ or _Kumar Khel_ form but a small clan, Samil in politics,

having its settlements in the extreme west of the Bara Valley and also

moving down to the Kajurai Valley to the west of Peshawar in the winter

months. Their fighting men number no more than about 800.

[Sidenote: Their Holy Places]

The _Zakha Khel_ owe their undoubted importance to their geographical

position in Afridi-land, rather than to the number of armed men they can turn out—probably not less than 6000. Their holdings stretch diagonally

across the Afridi country from the south-east corner of Maidan to the

Khyber Pass; they are the wildest and most turbulent amongst their

tribe and their land being unproductive they depend a good deal upon

raiding and blackmailing for their livelihood, are "the wolves of the

community," and since—at any rate up to recent times—"they lent no

soldiers to the ranks of the British army and had no pensions to lose,"

the Zakha Khels have always been more ready to give trouble than the

rest of their fellow tribesmen. They hold, moreover, some five miles of

the country lying on either side of the road in what Warburton calls

"the real Khyber proper," from the Shrine of Gurgurra (the sloe-tree)—where a small post is held by the Khyber Rifles—to Loargai in

the Shinwari country. Of this shrine, Warburton tells the following story

of how the Zakha Khels managed to remove the reproach which had been leveled against them, _i.e._ that their country

possessed none of the ziarats, or sacred shrines, to the memory of

saints or martyrs. "The Zakha Khel Afridis," writes Warburton, "bear a

most unenviable name as being the greatest thieves,

housebreakers,
robbers and raiders amongst all the Khyber clans, their word or promise
never being believed or trusted by their Afridi brethren without a
substantial security being taken for its fulfillment. Naturally a race so
little trusted were not fortunate enough to possess a holy man whose
the tomb would have served as a sanctuary to swear by, and thus save the
the necessity of substantial security. One day, however, a Kaka Khel Mia
came into their limits with the object of seeking safe conduct through
their territory to the next tribe. They received him with all politeness, but finding in the course of conversation that he was of
saintly character—a holy Kaka Khel Mia—they came to the conclusion that
he was just the individual who wanted to put their character for
truthfulness on a better footing. They, therefore, killed him and buried
him, making his tomb a shrine for all true believers to reverence, and a
security for themselves to swear by."

Oliver caps this story with another of the same character: "A Mullah was
caught copying the Koran. 'You tell us these books come from God, and
here you are making them yourself. It is not good for a Mullah to tell

lies'; so the indignant Afridis made another ziarat for him."

It is only quite within recent years that the Zakha Khels have taken to
military service, and even now the number enlisted in the regular Indian
the army is relatively small, the majority preferring service near their
homes and joining the Khyber Rifles. In politics the Zakha Khels are
Tamil.

The _Sipah_ is only a small clan, Samil in politics, and cherishing a
standing feud with the Aka Khel. Their main settlements are in the
the upper portion of the Bara Valley, with the Zakha Khel bordering them on
one side and the Kambar Khel on the other, while they also have
settlements in the Kajurai plain, where is their notorious rifle factory
at Ilmgudar.

Ranken defines the tribal limits in the Khyber Pass as follows: "The
Kuki Khels from Jumrud to where the Mackeson road begins; the Sipah
Afridis from the beginning of the Mackeson road to Shagai; the Kambar
Khel from Sultan Tarra to the white mosque of Ali Musjid; the Malik
Khel from the mosque to Gurgurra; the Zakha Khel from Gurgurra to the
Kandar ravine near Garhi Lalabeg; and the Shinwaris westward of

Tolkien."

[Sidenote: The Khyber Pass Afridis]

The above-mentioned six clans are known collectively, as already

mentioned, as the "Khyber Pass Afridis." The British connection with them

commenced as far back as 1839, when a Sikh force under Colonel Wade, and

Shah Shuja's contingent with British officers forced the Khyber—of

which the actual defile may be said to be in the hands of these

half-dozen clans. "In our earlier Afghan campaigns, they fully maintained

their ancient fame," writes Oliver, "as bold and faithless robbers, but

from the time Punjab was annexed, up to the second Afghan War, there

behavior was, for Afridis, fairly good. In 1878 some of the clans took

sides with us, and some with the Amir, necessitating a couple of

expeditions into the Bazar Valley," and during the two phases of the

the campaign not less than 15,000 fighting men were required to keep open

our communications with India by the Khyber route, despite the

the arrangement which had been come to with the clans bordering on the

Khyber, which will now be described.

When, in 1878, the Government of India called upon the

Commander-in-Chief to put forward proposals for the conduct of a

campaign in Afghanistan, Sir Frederick Haines offered the suggestion,

inter alia, that "a demonstration should be made early in the

operations of an advance by the Khyber, by encamping out a certain

the proportion of the Peshawar troops, making arrangements with the Khyber is

for their passage through the pass."[103] In consequence of the above,

Major Cavagnari was instructed to come to a friendly understanding with

the Khyber Pass Afridis, and to arrange for the passage of troops

through the defiles at certain rates. Major Cavagnari based his estimate

of the money payments to be made to the headmen of the clans, on the

sums paid by Colonel Mackeson for the same purpose during the latter

period of the first Afghan War; and he finally compounded with the six

clans of Khyber Afridis for a payment of Rs. 5950 per mensem, which sum

was willingly accepted. When, in September 1880, northern Afghanistan

was finally evacuated by our troops, the Indian Government, recognizing

the undesirability of maintaining any regular force in the Khyber,

expressed a wish to hand the pass over entirely to the

independent
charge of the neighboring clans provided some wholly satisfactory
the arrangement could become to for keeping the road open, and for
safeguarding the caravans passing to and fro between Afghanistan and
India. Early in 1881 a complete jirga of all the Khyber clans assembled
in Peshawar, and an agreement was arrived at whereby the independence of
the Afridis were recognized, and they engaged, in consideration of
certain allowances, to maintain order throughout the Khyber; the
The government of India reserved the right of re-occupation of the pass, and
was to take all tolls; the Afridis providing a force of Jazailchis paid
for by the Indian Government, and were to deal by a general jirga with
all offenses committed on the road. The allowances were fixed at Rs.
85,860 per annum for the six clans immediately concerned with the
policing of the past, and for the Shinwaris of Loargai; and a further
the sum of approximately the same amount was guaranteed by the Government of
India for the upkeep of the Jazailchis—since improved into the Khyber
Rifles—a body about 550 strong. As a set-off against these money grants

the tolls on caravans amounted to some 60,000 rupees per annum. The
allowances then granted are today substantially the same; the pass is
again in charge of the Khyber Afridis, and is again guarded, from Jamrud
to Lundi Kotal, by the Khyber Rifles, who have, however, been completely
reorganized, and are now a body 1700 strong, with six British officers.

[Sidenote: The Khyber]

Of that portion of the Khyber which is under our control the
following description is given by Warburton: "The main road from
Peshawar to Kabul passes through Jumrud, going almost due east to west.
After leaving Jumrud it passes through an easy country, having low hills
on the left-hand side, and about the third mile, it enters the hills at
an opening called Shadi Bagiar. A ridge from the lofty Ghund-ghar on the
left runs down to the road and faces a similar ridge coming down from a
prolongation of the Rhotas Range. The highway runs for a short distance
through the bed of a ravine and then joins the road made by Colonel
Mackeson in 1839–42, until it ascends to the Shagai Plateau on the left-hand side, and here Ali Musjid is seen for the first time. Still going
westward the road turns to the right, and by an easy zigzag

descends to

the stream and runs along its side, and below Ali, Musjid goes up the

waterway. The new road along the cliff was made by us in 1879–80, and

here is the narrowest part of the Khyber, not more than fifteen feet

broad with the Rhotas hill on the right hand fully 2000 feet overhead.

Still progressing, at about 400 yards from Ali Musjid, on the left-hand

side, three or four large springs issuing from the rock give the whole

water supply to this quarter. Between two and three miles comes the

Malik Khel hamlet of Katta Kushtia; soon after Gurgurra is reached,

and then we are in Zakha Khel limits in the real Khyber proper until we

come to the Shinwaris of Lundi Kotal, or more properly Loargai. The

valley now widens out, and on either side lie the hamlets and some sixty

forts of the Zakha Khel Afridis. Here, there is no stream, and the

residents have to depend on rainwater collected in tanks. The Large

Shinwari Plateau is some seven miles in length, and there is its widest

part. Just here above Lundi Khana, the old road was a very nasty bit...

From Shadi Bagiar to Lundi Khana the pass cannot be more than twenty miles in a direct line. When the first detachment of our troops returned

from Kabul,[104] they marched from Ali Musjid along the bed of the

stream, by Lala China, Jabagai, Gagri, Kaddam, 'the real gate,' and Jam,

villages of the Kuki Khel Afridis, to Jumrud; but Colonel Mackeson,

finding this way extremely difficult and unsuitable for guns and wheeled

traffic, made an excellent road from Ali Musjid to Fort Jumrud through

the hills, the same that we now use."

[Sidenote: The Trans-Frontier Khyber]

The trans-frontier portion of the Khyber route to Kabul is described by

Oliver as follows: "Over the Lundi Khana Pass, called the Kotal,[105]

the road rises by a steep ascent between cliffs less than 150 feet

apart, and down again till the Valley of the Kabul River is reached at

Dakka... At Jalalabad—ninety miles from Peshawar—the cross ranges of

hills are, for a change, replaced by a well-watered fertile stretch of

country, a score of miles long by a dozen wide, dotted with towers,

villages and trees; and where the Kabul River—that has all along had to

struggle through mere cracks—becomes a broad clear stream 100 yards

wide. Thence the route lies through a thorough

y unattractive country
again, over long stony ridges, across rocky river beds,
varied with an
the occasional fine valley like Fatehabad, or an oasis-like
Nimlah, to
Gandamak, which, by way of comparison with what is
beyond again, is a
a land flowing with milk and honey; for on by Jagdalak and
the Lataband
Pass, or Tezin and the Khurd Kabul, is a wild waste of bare
hills,
surrounded by still loftier and forbidding mountains. The
teeth
become more closely set together; the road narrower; the
stony ridges
change to bleak heights from 7000 to 8000 feet high, the
river beds,
deep valleys, or narrow defiles, like the fatal Jagdalak,
almost devoid
of verdure, and into whose gloomy ravines the winter sun
can hardly
penetrate—these are the outworks that have to be
negotiated before the
gardens and orchards, the bazaars and forts of Kabul, can
be
approached."

The _Aka Khel_ clan occupies the hills to the south-
west of Peshawar
between the Bara River and the country of the Adam Khel,
also the Bara
and the Warren Valleys. It was in the Warren Valley and
the house of
that firebrand among the border clergy, Saiyid Akbar, that

there was

found, during the Tirah expedition, the whole of the

inflammatory correspondence which had passed between the Afridi maliks

and mullahs before and during the Pathan revolt of 1897. This clan is

Samil in politics and can put 4000 armed men in the field.

[Sidenote: The Adam Khels]

The _Adam Khel_ clan is located in the hills between Peshawar and Kohat,

being bounded on the north and east by the Khattaks, on the south by the

Bangash, and on the west by the Aka Khel (their deadly enemies), and by

the Orakzais. They are one of the most powerful and numerous of the

Afridi clans, have a great reputation for bravery and can bring into

the field 6500 fighting men, who, moreover, are unusually well-armed,

with rifles stolen from our cantonments and with those they manufacture

themselves at their factories in the Kohat Pass. They are to a small

extent cultivators, but their chief occupation is carrying salt from the

mines; while the allowance they receive from the Indian Government for

keeping open the Kohat-Peshawar road is assistance to their revenues,

an allowance that has been paid them since the days of the Sikh

governors of Peshawar. The Adam Khels do not belong to

either of the two
great political factions. From the situation of the Adam Khel country,
and because their very existence is dependent upon their
trade with British territory, this particular clan is very susceptible
to a blockade and can consequently, be easily brought to terms. Nearly
all the trouble we have had with the Adam Khel in the past has been due
to disputes about the salt tax, or about the maintenance of a
the practicable road through the Kohat Pass. This shortcut from Peshawar to
Kohat has a certain strategic value; by this road the two frontier
garrisons are no more than thirty-seven miles apart, and only ten of
these are in the independent territory, while round by railway, via
Khushalgarh on the Indus, the distance is 200 miles. Two divisions of
the Adam Khels are the actual keepers of the past, and though we pay,
and have paid for years, a considerable subsidy, until comparatively
lately, we were not allowed to make a road, or even to remove the
boulders that obstructed the path. From about 1865 onwards the question
of the construction of a road practicable for wheeled traffic was
continually raised, and was as often dropped in face of

tribal
opposition. It was one of the main objects of the expedition of 1877,
but was given up by Lord Lytton to avoid "breaking the spirit of the
clan," who evinced their gratitude the year following—that of the Afghan
War—by threatening to close the road to us. This threat came, however,
to nothing, and the pass formed, throughout the campaign, an unmolested
and important means of communication between Peshawar and Kohat. Water
is very scarce in the past, the supply being dependent mainly upon
tanks.

During the risings of 1897–98, the Adam Khel remained perfectly quiet,
and troops constantly used the pass, through which at last, in 1901, a
metalled cart road was made.